Politics

Simon Adams

amicus

Published by Amicus
P.O. Box 1329, Mankato, Minnesota 56002

Printed in the United States of America at
Corporate Graphics International in North Mankato, Minnesota.

Published by arrangement with the Watts Publishing Group Ltd., London.

Library of Congress Cataloging-in-Publication Data

Adams, Simon.
  Politics / by Simon Adams.
      p. cm. -- (Media power)
  Includes index.
  Summary: "Discusses the media treatment of politics and politicians worldwide,
including issues of media pressure, biases, and scandals"--Provided by publisher.
  ISBN 978-1-60753-114-2 (library binding)
  1. Mass media--Political aspects--Juvenile literature. 2. Press and politics--Juvenile literature.
  3. Journalism--Political aspects--Juvenile literature. I. Title.
  P95.8.V38 2011
  302.23--dc22

                                                                        2009051449

Series editor: Julia Bird
Design: Nimbus Design

Picture credits:
                       0416
Alessandra Benedetti/Corbis: 11; Bettmann/Corbis: 18, 24, 37; Jim Bourg/Reuters/Corbis: 13.
Alexei Druzhinin/AP/PAI: 27; Peter Foley/epa/Corbis: 12; John Grainger/Newspix: 29.
John Henshall/alamy: 32; ImageWorks/Topfoto: 39; Nils Jorgensen/Rex Features: 26.
Yuri Kotchetkov/epa/Corbis: 17; Masatomo Kuriya/Corbis: 22; Danny Lehman/Corbis: 21.
Simon Marcus/Corbis: 35; Toby Melville/Corbis: 10; Jeff Moore/Empics/PAI: 31;
NBCUPhotobank/Rex Features: 30, Newsgroup/Rex Features: 34; M J Perris/Alamy: 8.
Olivier Polet/Corbis: 14; Altaf Qadri/AP/PAI: 19; Reuters/Corbis: 15.
Rex Features: 16; Jake Roth/AP/PAI: front cover; Sipa Press/Rex Features: 23, 25, 41.
Jim Sulley/epa/Corbis: 28; Sang Tan/PAI: 38; View China/Rex Features: 9.
Robert Wallis/Corbis: 33; William Whitehurst/Corbis: 40.

Every attempt has been made to clear copyright.
Should there be any inadvertent omission,
please apply to the publisher for rectification.

1212
32010

9 8 7 6 5 4 3 2 1

Contents

Politics
and the Media

The media plays an important part in all our lives. Most people watch television and listen to the radio, while many also read newspapers or magazines. Increasing numbers of people access the Internet through computers or cell phones. We live in a media world, and we are bombarded with news and entertainment every minute of the day.

Political Information

The various forms of media are all channels through which information is directed from its source to us, the public. One of the main types of information that we receive via the media is politics. Politics is the practice of forming, directing, and running countries or other political organizations, such as political parties. It concerns the complex relationships of people within a society, particularly those in authority. Above all, politics involves power and how power is obtained, directed, controlled, used, and abused in a society or organization.

Politics and Us

Politics is very important to our daily lives. It influences how our country is governed. It can work to change laws

Many people learn about politics from newspapers, although newspaper readership is slowly declining in most countries.

TV news and current affairs programs inform us of political events across the world.

and policies. It lays down the framework of rules and laws that we have to obey and the penalties we face if we break them. It also lays down the rules and behavior of our society.

Correct and Fair

Because politics is so important to all of us, it is important that the information we receive about it via the media is correct and fair. The media, however, has great political power of its own. It can influence politics and how we think about politics and politicians. This book looks at the relationship between these two powerful forces.

• Up for Discussion •

How do you learn about politics? By reading newspapers, watching television, listening to the radio, or via the Internet?

Do you think that politics is important to your daily life? In what ways?

Who Owns the Media?

At first glance, ownership of the media seems much less important than what it broadcasts. After all, most people watch television because they like the show, not because they approve of the owner of the channel. But media ownership is very important and can be very political, too.

Ownership and Control: TV and Radio

Ownership of the media varies from country to country. Most countries have a national broadcasting network or station, such as PBS (Public Broadcasting Service) or the BBC (British Broadcasting Corporation), that broadcasts television and radio programs as well as commercial networks. The national network often has an educational, social, or cultural role. For example, it may broadcast programs to schools and to minority groups or produce important programs that have a limited appeal. A national network is paid for through taxation or donations. Commercial networks are owned by private companies and make their money from advertising and selling their programs to other channels. This is why they mainly produce popular programs designed to appeal to large numbers of viewers who then attract advertisers.

The BBC was the world's first national broadcasting organization when it was founded in 1922. Currently, it is the world's largest broadcaster.

Newspapers and the Internet

Newspaper and magazine ownership is more varied, although many countries have a small number of private or commercial owners who own most national and regional newspapers. The Internet is far more open. Although a number of large international companies, such as Yahoo! and Google, run the browsers and search engines that help you to navigate the web, anyone can set up their own web site and publish whatever material they like, within the laws of the land.

Case Study: Concentration of Ownership

Ownership of the media can become important when it is concentrated into a very few hands. In Italy, business tycoon Silvio Berlusconi built up a media empire that included three national television channels, a number of satellite and digital channels, as well as some mass-circulation magazines. In 1994, he became prime minister of Italy, giving him control of the national RAI (Radiotelevisione Italiana) network. He now owns or controls about 90 percent of all free-to-view television channels in Italy and has a near-monopoly in broadcasting. This makes it very difficult for his political opponents to get their views heard on radio or television or present a case that the prime minister opposes.

Silvio Berlusconi is a politician and a media magnate with vast control over Italian television.

• Up for Discussion •

Does it matter that one man, such as Silvio Berlusconi, can control so much of what a single country reads or watches? How do you think ownership can influence what we see, read, or hear?

Fair and Balanced?

When we listen to the news, we believe that what we are hearing is being presented in an unbiased manner. We expect to be told the truth about a situation or event. But are we always right to trust the news?

Case Study: Fox News

Fox News Channel is a U.S.-based cable and satellite news channel owned by the media tycoon Rupert Murdoch. It first broadcast in 1986 and is now the number one U.S. cable news channel, presenting a variety of news and current affairs programs up to 15 hours a day. The channel's slogan is "Fair & Balanced" and boasts, "We Report, You Decide."

Rupert Murdoch poses with his wife, Wendi Deng. Murdoch heads one of the largest and most powerful media companies in the world.

Is it Fair?

Most TV news channels would claim to be unbiased and neutral in their reporting. Not all deliver on this claim, however. For example, throughout its history, the Fox News Channel has been accused of a right-wing or conservative bias in its reporting, its content, and its presentation of its programs. The channel has always promoted the ideas and beliefs of the right-wing Republican Party, and it attacks the more progressive ideas of the Democratic Party, now led by U.S. President Barack Obama.

Out in the Cold

Fox News owner Rupert Murdoch has rejected these claims of bias. He states that the channel "has given room to both sides, whereas only one [the Democrat] side had it before." Before the 2008 presidential election, Rupert Murdoch did try to improve relations between Barack Obama and the channel by arranging an interview with its most conservative

Barack Obama was one of several candidates for the Democratic Party's presidential election who refused to take part in Fox News debates because of the channel's bias.

commentator, Bill O'Reilly. Just hours later, however, another Fox News interviewer, Gregg Jarrett, threatened to "shut down the microphone" of a senior Obama advisor while she was on air. The channel maintained a continually critical view of Obama throughout the election campaign.

Government Support

Russian and Italian television stations are consistently pro-government in their political stance. They have been accused of slanting their reporting to present the government in the best possible light.

• Up for Discussion •

How do you identify bias in the media?

Is there any such thing as an unbiased news report?

A Different
Perspective

Much of the world's broadcasting media is owned by a few, mainly American, companies. Their television programs and related web sites are broadcast around the world, but the views they present and the choices they make as to the content and importance of news events often reflect a western outlook on the world.

Al Jazeera

In contrast, Al Jazeera is a media network based in Doha, the capital of Qatar, in the Persian Gulf. Its Arabic name means "the Island" as it currently is the only independent Middle Eastern news and current affairs station among state-owned and regulated stations. The station was set up in 1996 with a grant from the emir, or ruler, of Qatar. It began life as an Arabic channel, but it is now independent and broadcasts in both Arabic and English. It plans to set up an Urdu channel to broadcast to Pakistan.

The main newsroom of Al Jazeera broadcasts news 24 hours a day.

Al Jazeera has broadcast many exclusives, including videos of Osama bin Laden, leader of al Qaeda.

An Independent View

Throughout its history, Al Jazeera has broadcast views that dissent from the official views of governments across the Arab world. It also has challenged views expressed by western governments and media companies. In January 1999, it broadcast comments by critics of the Algerian government, leading that government to cut off electricity supplies to large parts of the capital, Algiers, to prevent the program from being seen.

Al Jazeera has also broadcast views and opinions that are hostile to Syria's involvement in Lebanon and that criticize the Egyptian judiciary. Most controversially, Al Jazeera broadcast statements by Osama bin Laden and other al Qaeda leaders after the 9/11 attacks on the United States, which offended many people in the West.

A Respected News Source

Despite this, Al Jazeera has become a highly respected media outlet. Many Arabic people see Al Jazeera as a more trustworthy source of information than the limited and censored news broadcast by their own government channels or the pro-western views of channels such as CNN (Cable News Network).

• Up for Discussion •

Do you think your national TV stations represent the world fairly, or do they have a bias in favor of your country?

Can a television station ever really represent the entire world?

A Free Press?

The Universal Declaration of Human Rights states: "Everyone has the right to freedom of opinion and expression; this right includes freedom to hold opinions without interference and to seek, receive and impart information and ideas through any media regardless of frontiers." But just how free is the world's press today?

A Citizen's Rights

The rights to speak freely and to read a free press are essential in a democracy. Together, they allow the people of a country to express different views and for those views to be made public so that others can be informed. In practice, a free press consists of newspapers and magazines that are free from government interference or censorship to publish whatever views and opinions they like, providing they keep within the laws of decency and are not offensive to people without justification.

A Broad Spectrum

In most western countries, there is a variety of newspapers, each publishing views from different political and social

U.S. voters exercise their democratic right to vote in the 2008 presidential election.

Case Study: Press Restriction in Russia

Anna Politkovskaya was a prominent Russian journalist and critic of her government who was murdered in 2006. Her killer has never been found.

Each year, the human rights group Reporters Without Borders issues the Worldwide Press Freedom Index. *It lists every country in the world in terms of how free its press is. The Scandinavian countries usually rank high, while North Korea, Burma, Vietnam, and China are near the bottom. Russia is also near the bottom of the list. The Russian government controls most television and radio stations and newspapers, although some local radio stations and a few business newspapers are independent. Journalists who oppose the government are often attacked: 49 have been murdered since 1992, making Russia the third most dangerous country for a journalist to work in after Algeria and Iraq.*

viewpoints—from the communist and socialist left to the conservative and religious right. In France, for example, newspapers range from the pro-communist *L'Humanité* across the political spectrum to the conservative *Le Figaro* and the Roman Catholic *La Croix*. In Britain, the range is from the communist *Morning Star* to the more conservative *Daily Telegraph* and *Daily Mail.*

• *Up for Discussion* •

Do you think a free press is important? Why?

Why do you think it is important that different political views find an outlet in the media?

Censorship

When we watch a television program or read a newspaper article, we know that decisions have been made about its content. A children's news program will feature news for children, while a small town newspaper will concentrate on its own region. But what if the content of that program or newspaper is censored?

Case Study: A Royal Scandal

One famous example of censorship occurred in 1936. British King Edward VIII wanted to marry an American divorced woman, Mrs. Wallis Simpson. The British king or queen, however, is also head of the Church of England, which opposes divorce. The government at that time did not consider it right that Edward marry a divorcee. British newspaper editors agreed among themselves to keep the story out of the news as reports might harm the institution of the monarchy. Reports and photographs of the couple's relationship were published in European newspapers, but wholesalers importing these newspapers censored the story before the papers went on sale in Britain. The British people only learned of the affair a few days before the king decided to step down from the throne to marry the woman that he loved.

The former King Edward VIII and his bride Wallis Simpson on their wedding day in 1937.

Good and Bad Censorship

Censorship is the suppression of speech or the removal of material that the censor considers to be objectionable, harmful, or sensitive in some way. Censorship is not all bad. Extremely violent material is usually censored as many people believe that it is harmful to watch and may incite violence. Pornographic material is usually censored, too. But in many countries, material that offends the government is also censored, sometimes by the government.

Political Censorship

Politically, many governments censor newspapers or block web site access to prevent people from reading about certain issues. The Chinese government, for example, heavily censors stories about the region of Tibet, annexed by China since 1950, where a campaign for independence is currently being waged.

• Up for Discussion •

Can censorship of the press sometimes be justified? If so, why?

What news stories, if any, do you think should be censored?

Exiled Buddhist monks lead a protest for Tibetan independence. Protests such as these are rarely reported in the Chinese media.

Open
Access

In the past few years, the media has been transformed by the arrival of the Internet and the World Wide Web. The web now provides an international source of information that is available to anyone with a computer and access to the Internet. Its open access presents opportunities, but it also causes problems.

What's on the Web?

Much of the content on the web is generated by commercial companies that want to sell you their products. The web also hosts official web sites from governments and political and other organizations, information and education sites from schools and universities, and—most recently—social networking sites such as Facebook and MySpace that bring groups of people together. Anyone with a minimum of technical knowledge can set up his or her own web site and put information on it.

Closed Web

The open nature of the World Wide Web allows information to flow freely around the world. This presents a problem to a government, such as China's, that restricts its people's access to web sites and clamps down on media that voices criticism of the government's policies. The Chinese government does not want its people learning about Tibet's struggle for independence from Chinese rule or about the Falun Gong, a banned spiritual movement it considers a threat. The government censors the web by blocking access to those sites and pages it dislikes or disagrees with, including web sites run by the BBC and the *New York Times*.

• Up for Discussion •

Should the web host sites that are controversial or contain misleading or wrong information?

Is freedom of expression more important than accuracy in a web site?

Users of this Internet café in Beijing are allowed to access only those sites that are approved by the Chinese government.

Virtual Police

One of the most important issues about the web, however, is that it is almost impossible to police. There is no worldwide censor to close down sites. However, individual governments can censor the web by shutting down or blocking access to sites that are illegal or pose a threat to a country's security. The web server that hosts or manages a site also has the right to close it down if the site is offensive in any way. In practice, that rarely happens, as most servers do not check every site they host unless there is a complaint.

Case Study: Getting it Wrong

One major problem with the web is that some of the information it gives out can be misleading or wrong. Before the 2008 U.S. presidential election, the web was full of personal sites and blogs that maintained that Barack Obama, the Democratic candidate, was Muslim and had attended a madrasa, or Islamic school, when he lived briefly in Indonesia. If that were true, it would have affected his chances of winning the election, as many U.S. citizens consider Islam to be linked to terrorist activities. In fact, Obama is a Christian and has never attended an Islamic school.

Spin

Most people try to present their actions in the best possible light, highlighting the good things while ignoring or downplaying the bad things. This is called "spin." In the world of media and politics, however, spin is much more controversial.

Spin and Spinning

The official definition of spin is that it is an interpretation of an event or campaign devised by a politician, journalist, or member of the press that seeks to change or manipulate public opinion in favor of those who would benefit most. The most obvious example of political spin is pointing out all the good facts about an issue, while hiding, or glossing over, its drawbacks. The media in many countries regularly

Case Study: "Burying Bad News"

One example of political spin is to delay the broadcasting of bad news until it can be released in the shadow of more important or favorable news. On September 11, 2001, the British government press officer Jo Moore e-mailed colleagues suggesting that "it's now a very good day to get out anything we want to bury," as any stories that reflected on the UK government would be ignored while the media concentrated on the terrible events of the terrorist attacks on the United States. This e-mail was reported in the media. After considerable criticism, Moore apologized but lost her job.

The 9/11 attack on New York's Twin Towers dominated the news at the time—so much so that many other stories were ignored.

Leading politicians, including French President Nicolas Sarkozy, rely on spin doctors to help them write and deliver their powerful and convincing speeches.

use spin by allowing only stories favorable to the government to appear on television or in the newspapers.

Public Relations

Spin can be dangerous, however, as it can undermine people's trust in a person or organization. For example, during the occupation of Iraq by the coalition forces after the 2003 invasion, some parts of the U.S. military suggested hiring public relations (PR) firms to put out and promote items of misleading or wrong information in order to increase public support for the war. This plan was never put into action, as government officials did not want to undermine the military's credibility and support by associating it with spin.

Spin Doctors

People who practice spin are often called spin doctors. Most modern politicians employ experienced spin doctors in their press offices to advise them on how to bend negative press coverage to their advantage.

• Up for Discussion •

Is it ever right to spin the news? When?

Is spin helpful or harmful to our understanding of politics?

The Right Look?

Very few have the opportunity to meet our political leaders in person. The closest we usually get to seeing them is on TV. But how are we influenced by what politicians look like on TV? Does their appearance affect the way people vote?

Face to Face

Every four years, U.S. citizens elect a new president or reelect the existing president for another four-year term. In the 1960 election, the two presidential candidates faced each other in four televised debates for the first time in U.S. history. The Republican candidate, Richard Nixon, was better known, as he had been vice president for the previous eight years. However, he had recently recovered from an illness and appeared haggard and unshaven, sweating heavily under the studio lights. In comparison, the Democratic candidate, John Kennedy, looked young, healthy, and vigorous. Nixon went into the debates as the favorite. But over the course of the debates, he was judged to be the loser and lost the presidential election by a narrow margin the following month.

John Kennedy (left) and Richard Nixon (right) face each other in a televised debate in 1960.

A Modern Contest

Forty-eight years after Kennedy's election, John McCain, a Republican, and Barack Obama, a Democrat, faced each other three times in televised debates. The two vice presidential candidates also held a debate. Both presidential candidates were well prepared, but neither was an outright winner of the debates.

The general media view, however, was that Obama had won the debates and came across as the more likable candidate. His popularity was no doubt boosted, like Kennedy's half a century before him, by his comparative youth and good looks. Obama was also, historically, the first mixed-race U.S. presidential candidate endorsed by a major party. He went on to win the presidential election in November 2008 by a wide margin.

John McCain and Barack Obama shake hands after the debates.

Public Opinion

In the 1960 and 2008 debates, the candidates were evenly matched and none of them struggled to answer any of the questions that were put to them. But did the people watching Kennedy and Obama in action change their minds after what they had seen? Or did the debates simply serve to confirm their existing views?

• Up for Discussion •

What can you learn from how a politician holds a debate on television?

Do you think that we should judge a candidate by the way he or she comes across on television? Why?

Questioning the Politician

Politicians regularly face television, radio, or newspaper interviews. Journalists ask about their policies and opinions, and sometimes exchanges can get quite heated. But should there be limits to these interviews? Should politicians be treated with respect, or are they fair game to journalists?

Paxman versus Howard

One famous television interview is always mentioned whenever politicians facing the media is discussed. In May 1997, British TV journalist Jeremy Paxman interviewed former Home Secretary Michael Howard on BBC's *Newsnight* program. Michael Howard had been responsible for prisons, but there had been a series of prison escapes. Howard had clashed with Derek Lewis, the head of the prison service, about the firing of a prison manager. Paxman asked Howard the same question 12 times: "Did you threaten to overrule him [Lewis]?" Howard did not give a direct answer but instead replied that he "did not overrule him," ignoring the "threaten" portion of the question.

Hostile Questioning?

The questioning made Howard look shifty, as if he had something to hide. The program did him great political damage. At the time, Howard was a candidate for the leadership of his Conservative Party, but he lost heavily in the first round of voting. However, he did go on to lead his party six years later. Many viewers felt that Paxman

Journalist Jeremy Paxman is feared for his tough interviewing technique.

Russian Prime Minister Vladimir Putin faces an interviewer from German TV channel ARD.

had been too hostile toward Howard and should have accepted his answer the first time. Government papers later released about the event gave some support to the answer that Michael Howard gave.

Was it Right?

Although the issues that gave rise to Paxman's questioning are now long in the past, the interview remains important. Michael Howard was a senior politician who had held one of the most important government positions of all—home secretary. He faced an aggressive journalist who was renowned for tough questioning and

made him look foolish. Is it right that the impact of this sort of questioning could make the general public lose faith in a politician?

• Up for Discussion •

Do journalists have the right to ask politicians any question they like? Why?

Should politicians have the right not to answer a question if they don't want to?

Talk
Radio

Talk radio is one of the most popular radio formats in the United States. It features politically opinionated hosts who present a live discussion on air about issues of the day. Their shows make no pretense to be balanced. Instead, they promote a particular political and social view and attack its opponents.

Lack of Balance

U.S. talk radio shows have been aired since the 1920s. Talk radio received a huge boost in 1987 when the Fairness Doctrine, which required radio stations to present controversial opinions and views in a fair and balanced way, was abolished. Freed from the requirement to present both sides of an argument, many presenters use their programs as a platform for their own political and social views.

Case Study: Rush Limbaugh

Currently, the most famous and successful talk radio host on air is Rush Limbaugh. His weekday, three-hour show is broadcast on more than 650 radio stations across the United States and has a minimum of 13.5 million listeners.

He uses his program to promote his conservative political views. For example, he campaigns against proposals to give illegal immigrants the right to become legal U.S. citizens and is a passionate supporter of capital punishment. In the 2008 campaign to choose a Democratic candidate, Limbaugh encouraged fellow conservatives to cross over to the Democrats and vote for the underdog candidate, usually Hillary Clinton, who was best able to challenge the front-runner, Barack Obama, for the Democratic nomination, in a plan he called Operation Chaos. His idea was to create havoc in the Democratic ranks by extending their hard-fought leadership contest right up to the party convention in Denver, Colorado, in August 2008, thus weakening the party to help a victory for the Republican Party.

U.S. radio talk show host Rush Limbaugh.

Alan Jones

Talk radio is mainly a U.S. phenomenon. Most other nations regulate their broadcasting stations to make sure they are politically balanced. However, it is also popular in Australia, where it is known as talkback radio. One of the most famous talkback hosts is Alan Jones, who hosts a morning talk show on Sydney's 2GB channel.

Like Limbaugh, Jones is highly politically motivated and uses his radio show as a platform for his conservative opinions and views. He has been embroiled in numerous controversies during his 20-year broadcasting career. He has been forced to answer to charges including defamation, racism, and being in contempt of court.

Radio talkback host Alan Jones has been awarded the title Australian Radio Talk Personality of the Year six times in his career to date.

• Up for Discussion •

Should radio be politically biased or neutral?

Could a talk radio host make you change your mind about an issue? How?

Politics as Entertainment

Politicians should be human and approachable rather than cold and distant. We expect them to be able to communicate well with people and to keep up with current affairs. But do we also want them to be entertainers, or does this just make them a joke?

A Stand-up Politician?

A week after he had been defeated in the 2008 U.S. presidential election, John McCain appeared on *The Tonight Show*, hosted by stand-up comedian Jay Leno. McCain told jokes about himself and his failed campaign. He was warm and witty and came across very well to the viewers. Many people said that if he had shown that side of himself during the campaign, he might have had a better chance of winning.

John McCain was seen as more friendly and approachable after his appearance on *The Tonight Show* in November 2008.

Case Study: Have I Got Politicians for You!

A long-running UK comedy show has led to questions about whether politicians should appear on such programs. Have I Got News for You is a weekly, hard-hitting quiz show about the news that includes politicians and comedians among its guests. Both Charles Kennedy MP, former leader of the Liberal Democrat Party, and Boris Johnson, a former Conservative MP and now mayor of London, have been regular guests. Charles Kennedy soon earned the nickname "Chat-show Charlie" for his willingness to appear. His career suffered as many thought he was too fond of being a celebrity and not serious enough to be a party leader. He was later forced to resign as leader when his party lost confidence in him.

The case of Boris Johnson is more complex. Johnson appears scruffy and disorganized, but his appearance disguises his intelligence. He became the target of many jokes on the program, but as a result of his appearances here and elsewhere, he soon became a household name. In 2008, he ran against the well-known mayor of London, Ken Livingstone, and made use of his popularity and familiarity to easily defeat the mayor. This gave Johnson control of the biggest city in Europe.

Boris Johnson is a shrewd politician who used television appearances to give himself a high public profile.

• Up for Discussion •

Can you laugh at a politician and still respect him or her? How?

Should there be a dividing line between politics and entertainment?

News Around
the Clock

National television and radio stations used to broadcast the news about four times a day. Today, that has all changed. News is now broadcast 24 hours a day around the globe on terrestrial, cable, and satellite channels. What effect does this have on politics?

Managing the News

In the days when a politician had only the fixed schedules of radio and television stations to respond to, he or she could make or respond to the news much more easily. Press conferences could be scheduled and statements released at a time to suit the politician, not the journalists. News coming in from abroad was broadcast only on the national channels, so responses to it could be timed to suit the politician. With only the national media to deal with, a national politician could remain, to some extent, in control of what was said and when.

Instant News

Today, major news stories that break in one country are broadcast around the world in seconds. Obvious examples concern Iraq or Afghanistan, when news of major U.S. or British casualties among the armed forces is immediately broadcast home. Major changes in the international financial markets or major political developments on the other side of the world can all be instant news.

The changes in the world's financial markets create important news 24 hours a day.

Case Study: Kolkata TV

Many 24-hour news channels are popular in the Indian subcontinent with 6 in Pakistan and 14 in India. One of the most controversial channels is Kolkata TV, which broadcasts news and current affairs, among other items. The channel reflects the political divisions in West Bengal, with a mix of right-wing and far-left political programming opposed to the long-running communist government in the region. Kolkata TV's 24-hour coverage of recent elections has made it the second most popular Bengali news channel.

The growth of TV ownership in India allows its people greater access to news and political debate.

Instant Politics

Faced with the constant barrage of news and information that continues 24 hours a day, politicians have now lost control of the news agenda. They must be ready to respond to questions from journalists at a moment's notice. If they decline to comment, their political opponents will gain the advantage and make them look foolish or as if they have something to hide.

• Up for Discussion •

How do people benefit from instant, worldwide news?

Do you think politicians should be required to respond immediately to the news? Why?

Newspaper Favoritism

Prior to an election, newspapers come out in favor of their candidate or party and urge their readers to vote for them. If their candidate or party goes on to win, they then claim some of the credit. But how much do newspapers really influence the voting decisions of their readers?

Case Study: Whose Victory?

The best-selling newspaper in Britain is the Sun, a popular tabloid newspaper owned by Rupert Murdoch. Throughout the 1980s, it heavily backed Margaret Thatcher and her governing Conservative Party and opposed the opposition Labour Party. In 1992, a new Conservative prime minister, John Major, faced the Labour leader Neil Kinnock at a general election. Kinnock was expected to win, but the result was a big Conservative victory. On voting day, the Sun filled its front page with the headline: "If Kinnock wins today will the last person to leave Britain please turn out the lights." The day after the election, the Sun boasted, "It's the Sun wot won it." But did it? Was the Conservative victory really due to one newspaper? In his resignation speech as Labour Party leader after the election, Neil Kinnock blamed the relentless opposition of the Sun for losing him the election. Many agreed with him, including the newspaper. But in fact, the truth may have been that voters did not really believe Kinnock was a suitable man to be prime minister, and they voted for the leader of the party with whom they were already familiar.

Neil Kinnock was heavily criticized by the *Sun* throughout the election campaign, and it ridiculed his ability to be a successful leader.

Newspapers can influence which party or candidate readers vote for but are unlikely to be the only factor in the decision.

A Matter of Preference

People read their favorite newspaper for different reasons. Some read it because they like its news coverage, while others enjoy its sports or entertainment pages. People often tend to read a newspaper that is close to their particular political views, but it does not mean that they will automatically vote for the party or candidate that their newspaper endorses. Most people make their own decisions about their political views and will vote for the party or candidate that appeals most to them at election time.

• Up for Discussion •

How can a newspaper influence how people vote?

Should a newspaper try to influence voting behavior, or should it be balanced between the parties? Why?

Getting it Wrong

When we read newspapers or watch the television, we like to believe we are being told the truth. We expect the writers and journalists to be experts and trust them to give us the correct facts. But the media can get things wrong.

Memorable Mishaps

The media attracts the public's attention with dramatic headlines and bold predictions. These ensure that people pick up a newspaper, tune into a radio or TV show, or study a web site. The danger with daring predictions is that they can be proven wrong. Economic forecasters often fail to correctly predict booms and busts. In politics, the media have been known to predict, and even report, important election results wrongly.

The 1948 U.S. Election

In 1948, the sitting U.S. president, Democrat Harry Truman, faced Republican Thomas Dewey in the presidential election. Most expected Dewey to win, as Truman was well down in the opinion polls, but Truman came out fighting. He embarked on two lengthy train tours around the country, speaking without notes and answering questions in a warm, relaxed manner. He appeared younger than his rival, although he was 18 years older and much tougher. "Give 'em hell, Harry!" people shouted at him. "I never give anybody hell. I just tell the truth and they think it's hell," he replied.

The Result

The result was a great surprise. Most newspapers and opinion polls thought that Dewey would win, but they did not do any late polling. This would have shown people changed their minds during the campaign and that large numbers of people decided which way to vote only in the last few days.

• Up for Discussion •

Should you believe everything the media says? Or should you watch or read with an open mind?

Does it matter if the media does get things wrong? Why?

They also failed to notice that 13 percent of those who said they would vote for Dewey stayed at home and did not vote. *Newsweek* magazine predicted a landslide for Dewey after it polled 50 leading political writers and did not find one who would vote for Truman. The *Chicago Daily Tribune* had to go to press before the results were announced and confidently published the story of the election under the headline "Dewey Defeats Truman."

The actual result was a decisive victory for Truman, who carried 28 of the 48 states and won a majority of 2.1 million votes. A victorious Truman was later photographed holding up a copy of the newspaper and smiling broadly, proving without a doubt that newspapers can get things wrong.

Harry Truman proved in 1948 that newspapers are not always reliable election forecasters.

National
or Local?

In some countries, newspapers and television or radio stations are almost national institutions. But a country the size of the United States or Russia is so large that it spreads over too many time zones for a national media to exist. Does this matter? Are we better informed by national or local media?

Local Variations

Local media offers people a more in-depth look at what is happening in their area or region. By focusing on a smaller area, the media can cover issues of local interest, including politics, in more detail and report events that the national media may have overlooked.

In countries such as Britain, Germany, and France, national newspapers and television and radio stations exist with their regional equivalents. The main British newspapers, for example, are sold in Scotland along with Scottish newspapers such as the *Scotsman* and local, usually weekly, newspapers published in each Scottish city and town. The same is true of TV and radio stations, including some programs broadcast in Scottish Gaelic for the minority who speak it.

In London, the *Evening Standard* and three free daily newspapers report on the issues close to Londoners' hearts.

Case Study: Reaching the People

The United States is too large for one newspaper to be relevant for every geographic area. The different time zones mean that evening programs in the East would be broadcast in the early afternoon in the West.

Americans are proud of their country, but they also identify with their own states and towns, which might well be thousands of miles away from the national capital in Washington, D.C. They also want to know the news, including politics, that affects their day-to-day lives. They may be less interested in political events in Washington, D.C. or the wider world.

As a result, there is no national newspaper in the United States, but a series of well-established regional newspapers, such as the New York Times, Chicago Tribune, and the Los Angeles Times, as well as numerous local newspapers that report city and state political news in addition to national stories. TV and radio stations are based in each state and major city and do not broadcast across the nation. However, many of the local stations are linked to one of the three major national networks—ABC, CBS, and NBC—whose programs they mainly broadcast.

Local news shows can feature more human interest stories than national news programs.

• Up for Discussion •

Have you noticed any difference in the way national and local newspapers report the news?

Do you watch national or regional television?

The Future

It is always hard to predict the future. That is especially true of the media, where new technology is being developed all the time. Politics also change as politicians come and go and new challenges emerge for them to tackle.

The Internet

One trend is certain. Newspaper readership is declining across the world as more and more people get their news from TV and the Internet. Politicians have turned to the Internet in particular to make their views known and to gain support. Most politicians have their own web sites and blogs, while many use their sites to raise funds for their campaigns.

In 2008, Barack Obama raised $657 million from individual donors—most of it over the Internet. He did not need to rely on public finance from taxpayers for his campaign and was the first presidential candidate to reject this money, which comes with strict limits on spending. His opponent, John McCain, raised only $324 million from individual donors and received $84 million of public funds.

Case Study: E-voting

The Internet is changing the way politics is conducted. Estonia uses the Internet to hold e-, or electronic, voting. It held the world's first e-vote for local elections in 2005 and the world's first e-vote for a general election in 2007. Other countries, such as Australia and Norway, are following suit, allowing their citizens to vote and participate in government via their computer rather than in person. However, the Internet is open to fraud, so it will be some time before the large democracies, such as the United States, follow suit.

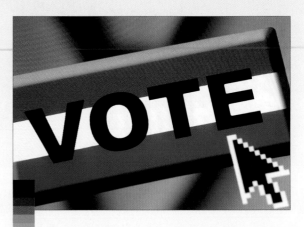

E-voting is practical and convenient for the voter, but it is also open to fraud and malfunction.

Close Relationship

It seems clear that in the future, politics and the media will become even closer. The importance of being seen and heard means that politicians need the exposure the media can give them more than ever, but politicians will also try to control how they are seen and heard as the media will be the main way in which they communicate with their voters and the country as a whole. The relationship between the two, and the issue of politicians owning or controlling the media, will be with us for some time to come.

German Chancellor Angela Merkel and French President Nicolas Sarkozy are skilled at using the media to promote their governments' policies.

• Up for Discussion •

Can you see elections in your town and country being conducted electronically in the future? What do you think would be the benefits of this? What about the drawbacks?

Who is in control—politicians or the media?

Glossary

annex To take over a smaller country or region and add it to a larger one, often by force.

bias A preference toward one side of a debate.

blog Short for web log, a web site usually run by an individual with regular updates providing news, information, and comments.

broadcast To transmit or send out a program on television or radio or via the web.

browser An electronic tool that enables you to find and view web sites and to handle e-mail and other Internet functions.

campaign A series of coordinated activities, such as speeches and broadcasts, designed to achieve a political goal.

censorship The suppression of speech or the removal of material that is considered to be objectionable, harmful, or sensitive in some way.

channel A television or radio service that broadcasts regular programs and forms part of a broadcasting network.

commercial Concerned with making money.

communist A person or organization who believes in an economic system in which everyone is equal and where all property is owned collectively by the people.

conservative A person or organization who favors keeping traditional customs and values and dislikes change.

defamation An attack on someone's character or name.

democracy Government by the people or their elected representatives.

endorse To offer support to.

free-to-view A television channel or program that can be viewed for free without a subscription or fee paid to the broadcaster.

human rights The basic rights and freedoms to which all humans are entitled, such as life, food, the right to work, and freedom of speech.

Internet The INTERnational NETwork of computers that are linked up via high-speed connections to share and exchange information and communications.

Labour Party British political party on the center-left of the political spectrum.

media Means of communication, such as the radio, television, newspapers, magazines, and the web, that reaches large numbers of people in a short space of time.

monopoly Exclusive control by a group of the supply of a good or service.

network A group of television and radio channels or stations linked by ownership or control.

politics The study and practice of forming, directing, and running countries or other political organizations, such as political parties.

poll The questioning of a sample of people to determine general public opinion.

search engine An electronic tool that enables someone to find suitable and relevant web sites and other material on the web.

socialist A person or political party that believes in equality and a fairer distribution of wealth and power.

spin An interpretation of an event devised by a politician, journalist, or press officer who seeks to change or manipulate public opinion.

tabloid A small-format newspaper often with many photographs and a sensational style of writing.

talk radio A phone-in radio show.

terrestrial television A television service that broadcasts its signals via a land transmitter.

Web, the Short for the World Wide Web, or www., the web provides an easy way to navigate around the Internet to find information.

web site Information collected together and published on the web and accessed by its own web address or URL.

Further Information

Books

Behind the News series (Heinemann, 2007)

Getting the Message: Political Messages and Propaganda by Sean Connolly (Smart Apple Media, 2010)

What's Your View? The Power of the Media by Adam Hibbert (Smart Apple Media, 2007)

Web Sites

www.pbs.org
The official web site of PBS, which offers shows on science, history, nature, and public affairs.

english.aljazeera.net
The web site of the Al Jazeera network. Includes political news and profiles.

news.bbc.co.uk/1/hi/uk_politics
Breaking news and political analysis from the BBC.

www.cnn.com/politics
News and opinion on U.S. and global politics.

www.foxnews.com
The web site of the U.S. Fox News channel.

www.rushlimbaugh.com
The official web site of radio talk show host Rush Limbaugh. It includes articles, views, and political commentary.

www.rsf.org/article.php3?id_article=29031
The Worldwide Press Freedom Index (2008).

Note to parents and teachers: Every effort has been made by the publishers to ensure that these web sites are suitable for children, are of the highest educational value, and contain no inappropriate or offensive material. However, because of the nature of the Internet, it is impossible to guarantee that the contents of these sites will not be altered. We strongly advise that Internet access be supervised by a responsible adult.

Index

Number in bold refer to captions to illustrations.

Explore the other titles in the *Media Power* series.